You Might Be a Senior Citizen if…

12 Lighthearted Clues You've Qualified for Senior Citizenship

By JP Collins

First Edition: 2025
ISBN: 9798276568812

CONTENTS

To my beautiful wife, Kathy, who will never, ever be as old as I am—and never a senior.

INTRODUCTION

There's no single moment when a person suddenly becomes a Senior Citizen. Ask ten people and you'll get ten different answers. Some swear it begins at 55, others insist it's 60 or 65, and a few say it's whenever AARP sends that first letter. Others say it's the moment the Walmart Vision Center tells you the senior rate applies—and you weren't even trying to claim it.

In truth, becoming a senior citizen isn't just about age. It's a journey highlighted by a collection of small, funny, perfectly harmless clues that start appearing when you least expect them. You catch yourself doing something familiar—something you once watched an older relative do—and suddenly you think, Wait… was that a senior moment? And then you laugh, because you know the truth: you've earned it.

This little book is a lighthearted look at those clues—the ones that make aging surprisingly fun. They're not signs of decline; they're signs of membership in a club most of us join eventually… and many of us join with a smile.

If you recognize a few of these, congratulations—you're finally slipping the bonds of middle age.

Welcome.

Long before active adult communities, heart-healthy diets, or senior-discount Tuesdays, the Greek statesman Solon is often credited with the idea that life unfolds in seven-year stages.

Each stage arrives with its own wisdom, responsibilities, and quirks — and if he were around today, I suspect he'd agree on one thing: the "senior citizen stage" is where the stories get funnier, the victories get sweeter, and the everyday moments become the best material of all.

READER CONTRIBUTIONS

Some of the lines in this collection came from friends, neighbors, and readers who were brave enough to admit they're "officially seniors." If you've got a great senior moment story, a one-liner, or a perfectly ridiculous observation we all relate to, I'd love to hear it.

Send your idea to:
clues@c-bgroup.com

Your submission might appear in the next volume.
(With full credit given, of course!)

#1

The Birth-Year Wheel of Doom

You Might Be a Senior Citizen If… you sit down to create an online account that requires your date-of-birth and end up spinning the birth-year wheel so far back you start wondering whether your year ever existed.

#2

Grocery Store Cardio

…your Apple Watch calls grocery shopping "moderate cardio" — and then sends an alert: "Cart wrangling detected. Please pace yourself."

#3

Home by 7:30

…you finish a long, laughter-filled dinner with friends, leave feeling happily stuffed — and still manage to be in your car and home by 7:30.

#4

Traffic Court Reality Check

…you walk into traffic court for a speeding ticket and instantly realize you're the only one without a face tattoo — or a TikTok livestream. Apparently, passing that slowpoke in the left lane is still illegal after all!

Contributed by Bob B.

#5

The Medical Briefing

...catching up with your buddies over drinks means the first twenty minutes are spent comparing surgeries, procedures, and new prescriptions — and nearly getting into a fistfight over whose orthopedic guy is the real miracle worker.

#6

The Christmas Inflatable War

…your young neighbors' holiday display includes giant inflatables, color-changing LEDs, booming music, and a full-on garage door projection of *Christmas Vacation* — and you think, "Back in my day, a candle in each window and a wreath on the door was enough to win Best Neighborhood Decorations — and who wants to blow up those giant inflatables anyway?"

#7

The Closet Phenomenon Conspiracy

…you've lived in at least three different houses in your adult life — but every closet shares one magical power: it mysteriously shrinks your clothes every year, with the miraculous exception of those trusty penny loafers, which always seem to fit just fine. At this point, you're fully expecting the Discovery Channel to air a documentary on the phenomenon next season.

#8

The Button-Down Microsurgery

…buttoning the tiny collar on your favorite button-down now feels like delicate microsurgery — because your fingertips just don't have the same feel or control they used to, and suddenly every button feels two sizes smaller.

#9

The Pill Organizer Arms Race

...there aren't enough pill organizers on Earth to keep up with your medication schedule: empty stomach, with food, thirty minutes later, lunchtime, mid-afternoon, with dinner, after dinner, before bed — and one pill that always disappears, either into that old 1970s shag carpet or, more often, into your slipper.

#10

The Disney VHS Archive

…you still have a shelf of Disney VHS tapes from your kids' childhood — even though the VCR hasn't worked since the Bush administration — and you're convinced Lady & the Tramp is still the closest thing to high art Hollywood ever produced.

#11

The Backup Camera Standoff

…backing out of a parking space means a wild game of "guess what's behind me," but you still refuse to buy a car with a backup camera — because your 2006 Honda Civic with 201,953 miles is "just fine," thank you very much.

Contributed by Ellen T.

#12

Writing the Book About It

…writing a humor book about becoming one requires frequent breaks — the kind that last for days, even weeks, just to recover from all that thinking. At this rate, Volume 2 might be ready by the time you turn 90… assuming you can keep your eyes open that long!

ABOUT THE AUTHOR

JP Collins is a Christian, husband, father, grandfather, Army Veteran, and lifelong observer of life's quieter comic moments. At seventy-two, he still insists he's middle-aged—a position his family disputes regularly and with great enthusiasm: "Grampa, you're just old." His knack for finding humor in the everyday realities of getting older inspired this lighthearted collection of senior citizen "signs," written for anyone willing to laugh at the small truths we all eventually recognize.

He lives in Georgia with his wife, Kathy–who, by all reliable reports is still smokin' hot.

ACKNOWLEDGMENTS

This book is, at its core, a collection of shared smiles. I'm grateful to the friends and family whose stories, humor, and honesty helped shape every page. Their willingness to laugh at life—and at themselves—made this project possible.

I'm also thankful for the modern tools that helped bring it together. The teams behind today's AI platforms, including ChatGPT, Gemini, and Perplexity, provided steady support in organizing ideas and refining this work.

And finally, I'm grateful for the faith that grounds me and for the example set by my parents, whose strength and conviction continue to guide me each day.

FUTURE EDITIONS

Future editions of this series will continue to arrive in sets of twelve—fresh chances to laugh at the moments we all quietly recognize. I'm genuinely looking forward to hearing from you and gathering your best senior moment stories, sharp observations, and the everyday quirks that prove we've crossed into "official" senior status. Eventually, these shared gems will come together in a comprehensive hardcopy volume—something our grandchildren can puzzle over as they try to figure out what in the world Grandpa or Grandma meant by half of this.

THANK YOU

Thank you for taking the time to enjoy a laugh with me.

If you found this book the least bit entertaining, I humbly ask that you take a moment to leave a star rating or a line or two of your thoughts online. It truly helps others find these stories.

And if someone in your life would love a chuckle (or needs one), feel free to share this book with them.

Got a fun idea or a senior moment story of your own? Send it to
clues@c-bgroup.com
It might end up in the next volume.

Made in the USA
Columbia, SC
20 December 2025

76468659R00025